THE PITKIN GUIDE TO

THE HOME FR

1939–1945

CHRIS McNAB

I n 1940, Britain stood bravely, but alone, against the full power of
Nazi Germany. Despite the unforgiving odds, the island nation more
than rose to the challenge, resisting the might of the German armed
forces even when most of Europe, from Poland to the French coast,
lay under German occupation. A defiant spirit meant that the British
not only inflicted the first major defeat on the Germans, at the Battle
of Britain, but also went on to be a key Allied power in the victories in
Europe and later in the Pacific against the Japanese.

There is an understandable temptation to focus exclusively on
the positive experiences of 'Home Front' life, such as the sense of
community. We must never overlook, however, the heavy price of
the Second World War paid by Britain – 382,000 soldiers and more
than 60,000 civilians killed. While the military campaigns unfolded
in distant parts of the world, at home millions of men, women and
children faced the formidable daily challenges of war. On the Home
Front, all the things we now take for granted – safety, food, fuel, clothes,
home and family – were disrupted
and threatened, and life became
very hard for the majority of the
population. Yet the courage, spirit,
humour and resilience of the
British people won through, and
it is for these qualities that the
wartime generation is respected
and remembered.

RIGHT: With labels round their
necks, a small boy and his sisters
wait at London's Euston Station
to be evacuated in August 1941.

A Country at War

Britain was a country in many ways unprepared for war. During the inter-war years, the nation's great empire began its slow decline, the financial burden being too severe for a nation hit by First World War debt. Then came the Great Depression – at home, 2.5 million people were unemployed by the end of 1930.

Adding to Britain's woes in the 1930s was a deteriorating international security situation, particularly the rise of Nazi Germany under Adolf Hitler. The British Prime Minister, Neville Chamberlain, attempted to manage Hitler's expansionist ambitions through a policy of 'appeasement', but this finally collapsed with Germany's occupation of Czechoslovakia in March 1939. The true extent of Hitler's intentions was revealed on 1 September 1939, when German forces invaded Poland. Two days later, Chamberlain announced that Britain was at war with Germany.

The period from September 1939 to April 1940 became known as the 'Phoney War', with little actual military activity. This situation changed profoundly with Hitler's invasion of Scandinavia, France and the Low Countries in April and May 1940, which resulted in the British Expeditionary Force (BEF) being ejected from the Continent by superior German forces. With the United States not yet in the war, Britain now fought on alone, albeit under new leadership – Winston Churchill took over as Prime Minister on 10 May. It seemed only a matter of time before Germany invaded Britain. Yet the RAF defeat of the Luftwaffe in the Battle of Britain (July–October 1940), and Hitler's new focus on the Soviet Union, saved the country from this fate. In its place, however, came the 'Blitz', the Luftwaffe's systematic attempt to destroy Britain's cities and industrial capability by night-time air attacks. It also failed, but from September 1940 cities such as London, Coventry, Sheffield, Portsmouth, Liverpool, Plymouth and Swansea endured massive,

RIGHT: A newspaper seller displays the sombre news that Britain is at war with Germany. The war declaration was made public in a radio broadcast by the Prime Minister, Neville Chamberlain, to the British public at 11.15 a.m. on 3 September 1939.

FAR RIGHT: A week into the newly declared war, a London housewife sets about painting a lamp-post black to meet the blackout regulations. For a time, even smoking outdoors was banned, the fear being that German aircraft would see the glow of the cigarette.

LEFT: A London shop worker places strips of tape in a tongue-in-cheek fashion across the plate-glass window of a shop. The thick tape would help reduce the chance of the window shattering from a nearby bomb blast.

BELOW: The fear that poison gas might be used by the Germans in a bombing campaign led to the mass issue of gas masks to children and adults. Here two wardens from the ARP Scheme fit a family with their masks during a home visit.

regular air raids that killed 43,000 civilians and left hundreds of thousands homeless – 375,000 in London alone.

The Blitz ended in May 1941, but four more years of war lay ahead. The suffering continued in the forms of rationing, family separation, tortuous working hours, periodic air attacks and, later in the war, bombardment by Germany's V1 and V2 missiles. The fact that Britain fought off German occupation, however, meant that in June 1944 the country could be used as the launch pad for the Allied invasion of Europe, which by May 1945 had brought the war against Hitler to an end.

'PUT THAT LIGHT OUT'

Shortly after the declaration of war against Germany, the British government implemented the 'blackout'. At night, virtually all sources of light – street lamps, domestic lighting, candles, car headlights, even cigarettes and lit matches – were to be either extinguished or hidden from external view, to prevent German air crew using them for navigation, a policy rigorously enforced by Air Raid Precaution (ARP) wardens. Home owners had to put up blackout curtains or shutters over their windows every night, and simply walking along a street became precarious. One serious consequence of the blackout was a high increase in night-time accidents (see pages 22–23). For this reason, the government relaxed the blackout policy slightly in November 1939, allowing a little more illumination for businesses and public services.

Sirens and Shelters

The Blitz (from the German *Blitzkrieg*, meaning 'lightning war') was a terrifying experience for Britain. An impending air raid was announced by the plaintive note of an air-raid siren, warning people to seek shelter. Many shelters, however, consisted of nothing more than domestic or commercial cellars, or any other similar underground space. Citizens in Liverpool utilized the gloomy crypt of St Luke's church, while the vaults beneath the Fruit and Wool Exchange in Brushfield Street, London, were crammed with up to 10,000 people in unimaginable squalor. Others camped in caves or woodland outside the city limits – Chiselhurst Caves in Kent virtually became home to some 8,000 people.

ABOVE: The Morrison shelter was designed to withstand two floors of rubble crashing down on top of it, protecting the occupants lying inside. The shelter was an option for those who didn't have an Anderson shelter or a deep cellar.

Above ground, there was always the Anderson shelter. This consisted of a large sheet of corrugated iron that formed the roof of a shelter 6ft (1.8m) deep, 4ft 6in (1.4m) wide and 6ft 6in (2m) long, set in a hole dug in the garden and covered with earth for blast protection. An Anderson shelter was damp, cold and miserable, but it could hold up to six adults and withstand all but a direct hit. Less reassuring was the Morrison shelter, essentially an iron cage placed inside the home, into which the family would crawl for protection in case the house collapsed. The Morrison shelter could hold up under tons of rubble, and saved many, although survival inside would no doubt be nerve-shredding. The third above-ground option was government-provided brick and concrete shelters, although poor build quality meant that many such shelters disintegrated under bomb blasts.

For Londoners, the largest shelters were the London Underground tunnels, but at first the government strictly forbade this use. Only as public anger rose, and citizens often forced their way down into the tunnels, did

SPIRIT OF THE BLITZ

Much has been made of the 'Blitz spirit', the qualities of cheerfulness and resilience that helped Britons mentally survive the bombing. There is certainly much truth in the notion. Even in bombed-out streets, people worked together to maintain the routines of normal life, and wryly humorous signs such as 'Open for business' were hung on shops that had windows and walls blown out. Yet it was not the full picture. Looting of bomb-damaged buildings was widespread (there were 390 incidents reported in London in just the first eight weeks of the Blitz), with many cases involving members of the emergency services, and opportunistic thieves found rich pickings in crowded public shelters. Murder rates also increased significantly from 1939 to 1942, as violent criminals realized that the death tolls from bombing provided the perfect cover to hide a killing. The Blitz spirit is certainly not a myth, but it is only part of the story.

ABOVE: A family in Manchester take delivery of their Anderson shelter. The corrugated iron structure had to be sunk 4ft (1.2m) into the ground and the roof covered with at least 15in (0.4m) of earth, to absorb blast effects.

LEFT: A London double-decker bus lies in a massive bomb crater in the centre of what was once a busy street. The Germans dropped a wide variety of ordnance on Britain, from small but numerous incendiary devices through to massive high-explosive bombs such as the SC 2000, which weighed 4,306lb (1,953kg).

the government relent. Eventually more than 170,000 people took shelter nightly in the 79 tube stations dotted across the capital.

Of course, shelter was not the only challenge of the Blitz. Those who had lost their homes to the bombing were often temporarily housed in overcrowded 'rest centres' run by local councils. Rehousing officers would attempt to find them new accommodation, but the process was terribly slow – in the first six weeks of the Blitz, 250,000 people were made homeless, but only 7,000 were rehoused. The citizens of Britain, and the emergency services, also had to cope with the violent death or injury of thousands of people. A single raid on Coventry on 14 November 1940, for example, killed about 600 people and injured 1,000 more, and gutted the city's famous cathedral. Yet through such adversity, the British people endured, probably more through communal support than any single government initiative.

Emergency Service Volunteers

Even before the war, there was a clear sense that any future conflict would have a serious impact upon civilian life, particularly in the form of air raids. In 1935 the government therefore issued Air Raid Precautions (ARP) circulars to local authorities, which in turn set up their own ARP units. From 1 January 1938 these units were made compulsory, and with the onset of war they became a central element of the broad Civil Defence (General) Services organization.

Once Britain was under actual attack, Civil Defence personnel served as an integral part of Britain's emergency services. Most of them were part-time volunteers, often putting their lives at risk purely from a sense of public duty. They performed a wide variety of emergency roles. The ARP wardens, for example, became responsible for reporting bomb damage, identifying the locations of unexploded bombs and supervising public shelters, and also assisting with casualty rescue and evacuation. (In London, there were about ten ARP wardens to every square mile of territory.) Other Civil Defence roles included building repair, first aid, rescue teams (typically men with experience in the construction industry) and firewatchers – the latter monitored the enemy use of incendiary bombs, reporting detonations to the fire service. Youth organizations such as the Church Lads' Brigade and Jewish

BELOW: A soldier of the Home Guard demonstrates a one-man cycle-powered ambulance, featuring canvas sides that could be rolled down to protect the patient from gas or smoke.

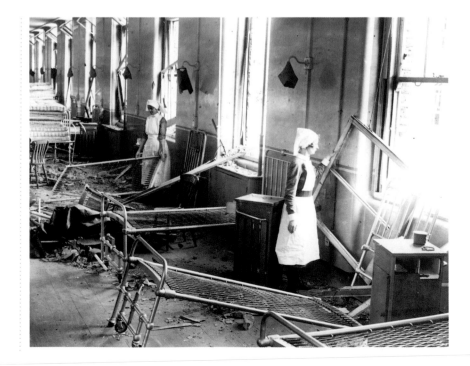

RIGHT: The emergency services themselves were extremely vulnerable to the effects of German bombing, particularly in inner-city hospitals. Here nurses begin clearing up a wrecked ward after a raid over London in September 1940.

Lads' Brigade provided thousands of adolescent messengers, who ran through sometimes bomb-blasted streets to take messages between control posts and wardens.

Fire services consisted of local authority fire brigades supported by the Auxiliary Fire Service (AFS), which was part of Civil Defence. The Blitz stretched these fire crews beyond their capabilities, exposing a lack of centralized control and poor, non-standardized equipment amongst the AFS. Fire personnel put themselves in nightly danger, tackling huge blazes with bombs still falling around them, and in May 1941 the government attempted to improve matters by combining all local fire services into the National Fire Service.

Another vital support organization was the Women's Voluntary Services (WVS). Established in 1938 by Stella Isaacs, the Dowager Marchioness of Reading, the WVS delivered a wide range of services, such as assisting evacuees, giving out emergency clothing, educating the public about waste, providing mobile canteens to rescue workers, helping those rendered homeless and feeding harvest workers. They were frequently in danger – 231 WVS members were killed during the Blitz. Indeed, a total of 2,379 Civil Defence workers had died serving their country by July 1945, a testimony to the fact that some individuals were prepared to give all to help others.

BELOW LEFT: London fire-fighters pour water into a blazing four-storey building during the Blitz. In the capital, the fire crews increasingly pumped water from the River Thames, although this resource was only available to buildings near the river.

BEWARE UNEXPLODED BOMBS

Unexploded bombs were a widespread hazard during the war years (and for some years after). From February 1940, responsibility for dealing with such ordnance fell to Bomb Disposal Sections (BDSs) of the Royal Engineers, and by September of that year about 10,000 soldiers were engaged in the work. Anti-handling devices introduced by the Luftwaffe in 1940 made bomb disposal lethally dangerous work – 490 BDS personnel were killed and 209 injured. By the end of the war, however, the Royal Engineers had made safe 45,441 bombs and 6,983 anti-aircraft shells. From 1943, they also had to clear some 300,000 mines emplaced on British beaches to protect against invasion.

ABOVE: A Bomb Disposal Unit team raises a 1,200lb (545kg) bomb from a crater. Lieutenant R. Davies, the team commander, stands on the bomb to control its swing as it is lifted, illustrating why bomb disposal was such dangerous work.

A Home From Home?

During the 1930s, concerns about future air raids led the British government to formulate a scheme for the evacuation of children and other vulnerable citizens from the big cities – the obvious targets for attack – to safer locations. Rehearsals began in the summer of 1939, but 'Operation Pied Piper', the evacuation of children, was enacted in earnest shortly after the outbreak of war in September.

There were actually four classifications of evacuee – blind and disabled people; pregnant women; women with dependent pre-school children; and school-age children. The evacuation of children was advisory, not compulsory, yet for millions of parents, genuine fear for their children's safety and moral pressure from the authorities meant an agonizing separation.

The evacuation process was often distressing and disorganized. Children were labelled like baggage, separated from frequently distraught mothers and sent off to unknown destinations on trains and buses. Typically they were moved to rural districts, where they were housed with strangers, largely through random selection processes. Many children arrived to discover that there was nowhere for them to go – Anglesey in North Wales expected the arrival of 625 children but actually received 2,468, and its experience was not unusual.

BELOW: Evacuation was recommended, not compulsory, but British Ministry of Health posters put moral pressure upon parents to send their children away. The benefits of evacuation are hard to judge, although the policy almost certainly saved hundreds of young lives in heavily bombed urban areas.

LEAVE THIS TO US SONNY — YOU OUGHT TO BE OUT OF LONDON

MINISTRY OF HEALTH EVACUATION SCHEME

EVACUATION DAY

Susan Waters, a teacher who took a party of evacuees from north London to Bedford, observed with distaste what occurred at the final destination:

The scene was more akin to a cattle or slave market than anything else. The prospective foster mothers, who should not have been allowed onto the field at all, just invaded us and walked about the field picking out what they considered to be the most presentable specimens and they harassed the poor billeting officer for the registration slips if they were to get the necessary cash for food and lodging from the government. Thus it was some hours before the children were all disposed of and those that felt they were going to be left behind were dissolved in tears and hadn't the slightest idea where they were going.

JULIET GARDINER,
THE CHILDREN'S WAR

LEFT: Evacuation required impressive levels of organization on the part of the authorities. Here police officers and railway officials are pictured helping 800 evacuee children onto trains in Ealing Broadway station, London, in September 1939.

BELOW: For many city children, evacuation brought their first taste of country living. Here boys from the East End of London get to grips with the wheat harvest in their new rural home.

Many children were lucky, being housed with kind families who looked after their emotional and physical needs. Others were less fortunate, finding themselves in unloving homes under harsh discipline. One boy recounted having his food stolen by the host family, and he was horsewhipped so badly he was eventually taken under the protection of local police. One study suggests that around 10 per cent of evacuees suffered some form of abuse. The evacuation was also a shake-up of British society. Poor urban boys and girls might find themselves living in rural affluence, experiencing a life they had not even dreamt about, while quiet village communities had to cope with an influx of city street language and behaviour.

The quiet of the Phoney War meant that by January 1940 about 60 per cent of evacuated children had returned home, against government advice. The fall of France (May 1940) and the Blitz, however, brought a second widespread evacuation, with 300,000 children rehoused. In addition, more than 2,600 children were sent overseas to locations such as Canada, South Africa and New Zealand, but the dangers to merchant shipping limited what was intended to be a major scheme.

Some children were to spend virtually the entire war as evacuees, although the majority steadily returned home in 1942–45, as the threat from German bombing diminished. For many ex-evacuees, the memories of that period, good and bad, remain vivid to this day.

FRIENDS FOR LIFE?

'[Douglas Monteith] was about my age and one of my friends. As we were leaving to go home at the end of the war in Europe, he and I took what we thought at the time to be a solemn oath; that wherever we happened to be we would keep in touch and meet now and again. We haven't seen hide or hair of each other since.'

WALLY SULLIVAN, EVACUATED FROM LONDON
TO WITHERIDGE, DEVON

Ration Books All Round

Wartime Britain was a place of austerity. Britain was an island nation, and by 1939 about 60 per cent of the country's food was imported. Germany's submarine war against merchant ships crossing the Atlantic literally had the potential to starve the nation into submission. In response, the government implemented a steadily tightening programme of rationing to control waste and excessive consumption.

One of the first goods to be rationed was petrol in 1939, and food rationing was introduced the following year. The system worked via a ration book, issued to all citizens. Each ration book contained coupons that could be exchanged for specified amounts of food. In addition, 16 unallocated points every month (later 20 points) could be used on foods outside rationed essentials, such as biscuits, fish and tinned fruit.

Food rationing reached its peak in August 1942, and certain items became very rare indeed, such as bananas, oranges and lemons. Government advisors and various 'agony aunts' in newspapers and magazines gave advice for creating supposedly sumptuous banquets from the most basic ingredients, but the reality was plain, repetitive meals. Furthermore, a ration book did not guarantee availability, so housewives commonly queued for hours for essential foodstuffs. Yet, ironically, the fact that every citizen received a balanced diet was actually an improvement on the inter-war years. Infant mortality dropped, as did incidents of malnutrition-related illnesses such as rickets.

From June 1941 clothing was also rationed, with clothing coupons issued in the same way as food coupons. Every adult received an annual allowance of 66 coupons. Of these, 26 coupons could go on a basic three-piece suit, or 11 for a simple dress. From 1942 Utility clothing was introduced, made from cheap cloth and designed to use minimal material (pleats and double-breasted jackets were amongst the features prohibited). Other rationed items came to include coal and coke (1 ton per month), and soap.

BELOW LEFT: By 1943, rationing was at its most stringent in the UK. Here two models show the latest in winter austerity fashions. Women were encouraged to adapt existing clothing with any scraps of material they could find.

BELOW RIGHT: A junior clothing ration book. Children were allocated more clothes' points than adults, to allow for their growing out of their outfits. Even handkerchiefs were rationed and could be purchased with 1 point.

LIVING ON RATIONS

Food restrictions were introduced in January 1940: butter, sugar and bacon were the first items to be rationed, with others following suit as the months went by. Although amounts were to vary depending on what was available, when rationing was at its height, a typical allowance per adult per week was:

1 egg (and 1 pack dried egg monthly)
2oz (55g) cheese
2oz (55g) tea
2oz (55g) butter
4oz (115g) cooking fat/margarine
4oz (115g) bacon/ham
8oz (225g) sugar
12oz (350g) sweets (monthly)
1lb (450g) jam (every one or two months)
3 pints (1.5 litres) milk
1s 2d (6p) meat (rationed by price not weight)

For those with enough money and the right contacts, goods could be purchased illegally outside the rationing system via the black market. Black market trading became a huge underground enterprise, with most people at some point acquiring illicit goods, whether it be an extra gallon of petrol or a cooked ham. The government imposed heavy penalties on those caught selling goods illegally, including a £500 fine and two years' imprisonment. It also issued many guilt-inducing posters, encouraging citizens to refrain from black market deals. Yet many people who lived during the war remember the black market being as much a part of life as rationing itself.

For all the hardship, rationing and shortages certainly brought out ingenuity in the British people. Housewives became adept at making or modifying clothing, utilizing any old scrap of material, and applying gravy browning to legs to simulate the effect of stockings. Although few things were in abundance (potatoes being a weary exception), people still managed to survive.

ABOVE: A typical ration of butter, eggs, sugar, tea, cooking fat, jam, meat and sweets allocated to each adult every week during the war years. Although the ration was basic, combined with vegetables it actually provided all the necessary calories, vitamins and minerals for good health.

Informing the Public

In wartime Britain, all propaganda activities were the responsibility of the Ministry of Information (MOI), which was established on 4 September 1939, the day after Britain declared war (although the organization had secretly been in planning since 1935). The MOI took charge of managing the flow of public information about the war, accentuating the positives and, as much as possible, downplaying the negatives. It also oversaw information campaigns, issuing cautionary publicity about the dangers of spies, waste, the black market, unnecessary journeys and other perils, while promoting courage, self-sufficiency and resourcefulness.

The MOI was a busy department as it had to monitor all major media outlets – cinema (mainly newsreels), radio and newspapers – as well as commission dozens of artists and other creative individuals to produce propaganda materials. In 1942 alone it spent £4 million on propaganda activities. In addition, its Home Intelligence Division collected information on the state of British morale and public responses to campaigns, feeding its conclusions back to the government.

For the British people, propaganda became omnipresent, although it never reached the manipulative and distorting levels experienced in Nazi Germany. Posters bore morale-boosting messages such as: 'Your courage, your cheerfulness, your resolution, will bring us victory'; 'The attack begins in the factory' (encouraging worker output); and 'Your Britain – fight for it now'. Many other

ABOVE: An important part of daily life as a family was gathering round the wireless – a bringer of latest news bulletins from the battlefront, and also entertainment.

RIGHT: Government information campaigns frequently focused on the dangers of spies, cautioning the British people to be careful about what they said in public. The fear was that, for example, a casual comment about a husband soldier on deployment would give away military secrets.

ENEMY EARS are listening

WARTIME CARTOONS

Some of the most powerful artistic images of the Second World War were created by Britain's cartoonists. One of the greatest was undoubtedly David Low, whose biting satirical cartoons featured in the *Evening Standard* newspaper from 1927 until 1950. During the war, Low drew cartoons that could be funny, uplifting or unnerving. In a typical cartoon, dated 18 June 1940, a single British soldier stands on a stormy English coastline, shaking his fist at enemy aircraft approaching in dark skies. The caption, 'Very well, alone', sums up both the disquiet and resistance of the British people following the fall of France. Other influential cartoonists included Sidney Strube, E.H. Shepard and Philip Zec. While their cartoons weren't always approved by the government, for the British people they represented the nation's eccentricity, individuality and courage at their best.

BELOW: Cartoonist David Low had the ability to sum up the mood of the nation. Here, in one of his most famous cartoons, he depicts the British government mobilizing behind the figure of Winston Churchill.

ALL BEHIND YOU, WINSTON

ABOVE: This poster from the Ministry of Fuel and Power advised people about ways to conserve energy in the home and at work. In the pre-nuclear age, Britain was acutely dependent on coal for most of its needs for power supply.

posters delivered specific warnings, instructions or recommendations, including: 'Careless talk costs lives!' (a warning about spies listening to militarily useful conversations); 'Save kitchen waste to feed the pigs'; and 'Don't take the squander bug when you go shopping'.

On the radio and via the cinema newsreels, the MOI tried to provide genuine information about what was happening without breeding pessimism. Churchill's stirring oratory (see page 31) was always popular material, as were stories of individual heroism and British pluck. The MOI would also advise film-makers about appropriate subject matter for movies, favouring those that raised themes of British heroism such as *In Which We Serve* (1942), *We Dive At Dawn* (1943) and *The Way Ahead* (1944). Documentary movies like *Target for Tonight* (1941) also gave the public a thoroughly edited insight into the reality of combat.

Early MOI efforts were heavy-handed and poorly coordinated, and not always well-received by the media or the public – one letter written to the MOI in 1940 stated that the author was 'so bewildered that I do not know what to believe'. Yet, over time, blatant propaganda became quieter as the government realized that in a time of war what the public wanted more than anything else was good information.

A Changing Workforce

Between 1939 and 1945 the material demands of war radically reshaped the nature of British industry. The war was insatiable for ever-greater volumes of weapons, aircraft, ships and other equipment, so the working lives of millions of Britons had to change to satisfy this need.

A fundamental challenge was the availability of labour. At the peak of conscription, more than 20 per cent of the British workforce were in the armed services, a severe gap to plug. In May 1940 the Labour politician Ernest Bevin was appointed Minister of Labour, with overall authority for British manpower allocation and mobilization under the Emergency Powers (Defence) Act. Bevin is chiefly remembered for two policies. The first was the creation of the 'Bevin Boys', young men conscripted into the mining industry instead of the armed forces. The second was the mass mobilization of women (who had previously taken a relatively minor role in the workforce), using them to handle roles traditionally performed by men. In 1941 many women aged between 18 and 30 (later raised to 50) were conscripted into essential vocations such as armaments and aircraft production or agriculture, adding a further 1.4 million workers to British industry.

In total, some seven million citizens were diverted or conscripted into war production by 1943. Many non-military manufacturers also switched to military products – the Nuffield Organisation went from making Morris cars to manufacturing Supermarine Spitfires, while the Slazenger sports-equipment producer began making items such as stocks for Bren machine-guns.

For the workforce the hours were long and hard, but the results were evident. In 1940 British factories produced 15,000 aircraft and 52 warships; in 1942 those figures were 24,000 aircraft and 114 warships. Production of ammunition went up fivefold in the same period, as did outputs of armoured vehicles. In balance, increases in British manufacturing were partly offset by the massive decrease in imports into the country.

RIGHT: Hundreds of British factories turned themselves over to war production between 1939 and 1945. Here we see workers fitting electrical components into the nose sections of Lancaster bombers.

The British government also encouraged its citizens to undertake fundraising activities to buy military equipment. Individual communities ran their own versions of nationwide campaigns with catchy titles like 'Wings for Victory Week', 'Warship Week' and 'War Weapons Week'. These activities mainly involved encouraging people to put their money into National Savings programmes, principally Savings Certificates, Defence Bonds and Post Office Savings Accounts. By doing so, investors not only received interest on their savings but also had the reassurance that their money would be used for weapon purchases. The campaigns, run like miniature festivals, raised significant amounts of cash. Leeds' 'Wings for Victory Week' alone raised £7.2 million to purchase dozens of fighters and bombers for the RAF.

The mobilization of British industry was overall a huge success for the nation. Through long hours of work the British civilian population largely ensured that their soldiers abroad had the equipment to keep on fighting.

BELOW: The mass conscription of women into industry was essential for British manufacturers to meet their production outputs. It also brought females into occupations traditionally reserved for men – here a woman works on an ammunition production line.

BEVIN BOYS

Although coal mining was a critical industry, by 1943 its workforce had been depleted by some 36,000 miners entering the armed services. In response, Ernest Bevin introduced conscription into the mines, one in ten men aged 18–25 selected for National Service being diverted into mining work. For the 'Bevin Boys' sent down the mines, life consisted of long hours enduring some of the worst working conditions in industrial Britain. Fatal or serious accidents were commonplace, and during the winter months miners could go for weeks on end without seeing daylight. Short-lived strikes became frequent – indeed, more than two million working days were lost to mining disputes. Yet the endurance of the Bevin Boys, and of the regular miners, ensured that Britain still maintained the coal supplies to power the nation.

ABOVE: Problems with finding enough men to work in the mines led to a government appeal for teenage volunteers. Here we see a group of boys beginning their training at Markham Main Colliery near Doncaster.

ABOVE: Fundraising campaigns raised millions of pounds from the public for the purchase of military weapons. Here the residents of Criccieth in Wales show that their efforts during 'War Weapons Week' have reached the £11,000 mark.

Feeding the Nation

Food production was another pressing issue for wartime Britain. The nation had been heavily dependent on food imports before the war, but by 1940 they were threatened by the German U-boat war against the Atlantic supply convoys. (Pre-war, British farmers produced only about 35 to 40 per cent of the nation's food.) In a similar way to the mining industry, agriculture was depleted by its workers joining the armed services.

It was vital that Britain increase its domestic levels of food production. To this end, millions of acres of unused land were converted to agricultural use, including 10-million acres (4-million hectares) of virgin grassland, primarily for growing wheat and potatoes. The Ministry of Food also strictly controlled the prices of those goods that were still being imported, meaning that UK farmers could take their produce to market and receive a good price for it. By contrast, if farmers did not modify their practices or maximize output along lines demanded by the government, they were at risk of having their farms managed by the state.

RIGHT: Work conditions for the 'land girls' could be extremely tough, with long hours of toil in the fields. Here women harvest sea kale at dawn. The leaves would be packaged immediately and sent for sale in the morning markets.

WOMEN'S LAND ARMY

The Women's Land Army (WLA) had its origins in the First World War, but it was reinstated in mid 1939. At first it relied entirely on female volunteers, who served in a variety of agricultural labour roles. Eventually, however, a conscription system was introduced that took the WLA to a total strength of 80,000 workers. Life for the 'land girls' was grimy and backbreaking, especially for those women pulled from city life and sent to work picking potatoes, harvesting crops and ploughing fields for up to 50 hours a week. A specialist force of the WLA was the Timber Corps, which made wooden props to hold up coalmine seams.

DIG FOR VICTORY ANTHEM

As part of the 'Dig for Victory' campaign, the government broadcast memorable songs on the radio. The lyrics to one of them were:

> Dig! Dig! Dig! And your muscles will grow big
> Keep on pushing the spade
> Don't mind the worms
> Just ignore their squirms
> And when your back aches laugh with glee
> And keep on diggin'
> Till we give our foes a wiggin'
> Dig! Dig! Dig! to Victory!

LEFT: This famous poster was part of the 'Dig for Victory' campaign, launched by the British government in 1939. By 1943, more than a million tons of vegetable produce were being grown privately in the UK in gardens and allotments.

To solve the manpower problem the government largely turned to women, and particularly the labour forces provided by the Women's Land Army (WLA). Thousands of women became agricultural labourers, keeping produce flowing from field to market. Another major strand in the government's attempts to encourage food production was the 'Dig for Victory' campaign. Quite simply, this attempted to turn Britain into a nation of amateur farmers, growing their own vegetables and keeping rabbits, chickens, pigs and other manageable livestock. Public parks and private gardens were converted into small allotments (1.4 million by the end of the war), which produced more than a million tons of vegetables annually. By the time the war was over there were 7,000 'Pig Clubs', groups of people who contributed time and money to buying and raising a pig for eventual slaughter. (Pigs were ideal livestock, as they could be fed on kitchen waste.) Rabbits and chickens could be bred for meat, and the latter also produced eggs, those most valued of wartime foods.

ABOVE: 'Pig Clubs' became a popular way of adding more meat to the ration. Here firemen of an Auxiliary Fire Service (AFS) station, who together have formed the Wyse Pig Club, show off proudly some of their livestock.

Britain's wartime agricultural revolution was a great success. The nation's dependency on imports dropped massively, while total home food production almost doubled. Although the diet of the people was basic, it was sufficient to ensure that the nation stayed properly fed.

A Woman's Place

For all its hardship, the war gave many women the chance to experience independence and self-sufficiency. Twenty-year-old Nina Hibbin, for example, joined the Women's Auxiliary Air Force (WAAF) and trained as a mechanic, eventually servicing Spitfires for combat squadrons. Other women manufactured ammunition and weapons, or drove tractors on farms. Some worked as railway mechanics or motorcycle messengers. Moreover, hundreds of thousands of women experienced wage-earning for the first time in their lives, no longer being dependent on a husband's salary or wishes.

RIGHT: Seven sisters from the same family are seen here working in a munitions factory in Enfield in 1942. Such employment was physically demanding, but it also brought more financial independence to thousands of women, something many had never experienced before.

BELOW: Women of the Auxiliary Territorial Service (ATS) man a sound locator unit, which used audible noise from enemy aircraft to guide searchlights and anti-aircraft guns. In such roles, ATS women were exposed to the full force of German bombing.

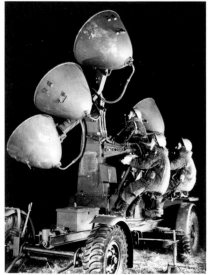

LIFE IN THE ATS

Mrs Margaret Ward remembers life in the ATS, which she joined as a young woman in 1941:

Although most of us would like to have been drivers, our hopes were soon dispelled – 'no drivers wanted'. I decided I would like to join a gun site as Radar Operator. At that time we were called Gun Operators, [or] 'Gun Layers' .... We were kept very busy and when on duty had to be ready for action at any time of day or night. One day during daylight a bomber flew fairly low, I think he had been hit and was going down into the sea, but he dropped his bombs and one fell on our gun site. Nobody was hurt, the bomb had fallen where all of our cables were buried, the transmitter unit was full of shrapnel holes, but the girls were OK. One got mentioned in Despatches because she had remembered to turn the power off.

Yet although women did a man's work, their wages were nevertheless kept below those of a man doing the same job. In textile work, a woman in 1942 would take home £2 3s, while a man pocketed £4 4s. A woman's day also extended well beyond finishing her shift, which could last for 10 or 12 hours – she was still expected to maintain the home, do the shopping and look after the children once she had left the factory. The problem became so acute that from late 1941 women were often given shorter working hours so they could fulfill their domestic chores.

As well as taking on industrial roles, women could join the armed services. The three major postings for women were into the WAAF, the Auxiliary Territorial Service (ATS) and the Women's Royal Naval Service (WRNS, known as the Wrens). Although women were not sent directly into combat, their work was essential and often dangerous. In the WAAF, as well as cooking and clerical duties, women were also found in frontline technical roles such as helping operate radar stations and manning fighter operations rooms. ATS women drove lorries, and manned searchlights and anti-aircraft guns (the only procedure they weren't allowed to perform was to pull the firing lanyard), while Wrens not only commanded harbour launches, but also performed duties that included loading munitions and signalling.

Many women found the war personally liberating, but we must not overstate the benefits. Women with children had to endure the terrors of attempting to protect their offspring from the bombing, not always successfully. For numerous women there was always the dread of the infamous War Office telegram informing them that a husband, brother or father had been killed in a far-off land. For married women in particular, the loss of a husband meant that they would have to cope on their own indefinitely.

Wartime Childhoods

Many children, particularly boys, felt a rush of excitement on declaration of war, looking forward to some drama in lives that were frequently predictable and drab. Yet the experience of war itself could quickly crush such optimistic enthusiasm.

Separation from parents and siblings, caused by either evacuation or death, inflicted a lifetime of psychological trauma on thousands of people. Among evacuees, bed-wetting from anxiety was common, which in less enlightened times could result in harsh punishments. Being orphaned by the bombing also had effects that went well beyond the war years. About 10,000 children, many of them wartime orphans, were forcibly sent to Australia during the 1940s and 50s, often to experience years of abuse at the hands of Church-run institutions.

ABOVE: From 1939 school days were punctuated by regular air-raid drills, teaching the children to move swiftly into nearby shelters. Here children in Southgate, London, emerge from a series of concrete shelters after a practice alarm.

RIGHT: A wistful child stands on sandbags and stares through the window of a London toyshop. For girls, dolls could be purchased wearing military uniforms, such as those of the ATS or WAAF, as well as various period outfits.

SUFFER THE CHILDREN

One of the great horrors of the Home Front was the death of children in air raids. In total, 7,736 children were killed in Britain during the war, and another 7,662 were wounded. Some incidents shocked even a war-hardened nation. On 20 January 1943, 38 schoolchildren were killed at Sandhurst Road School in Catford, south London, which was attacked by a German aircraft – deliberately so, according to eyewitnesses. On 3 March 1943, a panic stampede amongst people taking shelter in Bethnal Green tube station resulted in 173 people being trampled or crushed to death, 62 of them children. Such incidents provoked widespread public grief. Indeed, such was the government's fear of generating panic that it did not publish its enquiry into the Bethnal Green incident until 1945.

Even for those children who did stay with parents, wartime life was typically austere. Toys became increasingly scarce, affected by industrial restrictions on the use of plastics, rubber and wood. Indeed, the availability of new toys in the shops dropped by 75 per cent between 1939 and 1945, making Christmases and birthdays rather unpromising events. Those toys that remained were typically home-made or were prohibitively expensive. Amongst the militaristic boys, lead soldiers, tin fighter aircraft, model guns and tanks, and war-themed jigsaws and board games remained popular, while for girls rag dolls were an age-old favourite. For pre-school children, very little was available, and problems with wood supplies meant that mothers experienced severe shortages of cots for newborns. The austerity also extended to sweets, which were of limited availability and range, and clothing for all ages. Some relief, however, came with the eventual arrival of American forces in Britain, who brought with them luxuries from home which they frequently showered on imploring children.

Education was also disrupted on the Home Front. In all schools across the country, the first sign of conflict was the issuing of gas masks to every child and the regular practice of air-raid drills. Schools themselves suffered from evacuation policies, either emptying as their pupils were relocated or expanding hugely as they received evacuees. In potentially dangerous urban areas, many children received no schooling at all – a report from April 1940 estimated that only 50 per cent of children were in full-time education. Many of those children not in school were forced to take demoralizing domestic work, or drifted to the margins of society to become involved in crime. By the end of 1940, juvenile crime amongst 5–14 year-olds had risen by 41 per cent, and by 22 per cent for those between 14 and 17. Child cruelty cases also doubled between 1939 and 1944, a sad counterbalance to the idea of Britain's 'finest hour'.

ABOVE LEFT: Toddlers descend into a concrete air-raid shelter in 1940. Evacuations, air-raid training, shortages of books and stationery supplies, and many other wartime issues had a tremendously disruptive effect on schooling.

ABOVE RIGHT: Despite the trials of war, children could still find moments of levity and fun. Here a group of children in the East End of London enjoy an ice cream, despite having endured a bombing raid the previous night.

HAVE A BANANA

'Very occasionally "luxury" goods came in from overseas. When there was a shipment of bananas, word got round and all the women queued up for them. My mother was very eager for me to try them, as I never had, but it was a strange taste to a palate unused to them, and I didn't like them. My classmates all reported the same. But my mother didn't give up: she would often tell me how much I would like this or that food when I would eventually be able to try it.'

PAT CRYER, WHO WAS A CHILD IN EDGWARE, NORTH LONDON, DURING THE WAR

Travel Chaos

People's ability to travel from one place to another was severely curtailed during the war. It was also, thanks to the blackout, made significantly more dangerous, particularly for motorists and pedestrians. In the early months of the blackout, drivers travelling at night were only permitted to use dimmed sidelights. The result was appalling: a total of 8,000 people died in road accidents in 1939 alone (in 1938 the figure was 5,570), and the fatalities climbed to 9,000 in 1941. An article by Wilfred Trotter, the King's surgeon, was published in the *British Medical Journal* on 17 February 1940, in which he said: 'Deaths by violence on the roads rose in the first month of the war from 500 to 1,100. Thus by sitting quietly at home Hitler's air force was able to kill 600 British citizens at a cost to itself of exactly nothing.'

Eventually the government had to act to reduce the spiralling death toll. Measures such as painting kerbs white helped a little, but cars were also permitted to use dipped headlights, if the lamps were fitted with slit covers that dimmed the light even further. A night-time speed limit of 20mph (32kph) was also introduced. Vehicle accidents therefore declined from 1942, although levels of fatalities remained worryingly high.

Despite the high rate of accidents, it became a challenge to even run a car, let alone own one. Petrol rationing and other austerities reduced private car ownership from 2 million cars in 1939 to about 800,000 in 1942, when petrol was completely withdrawn from domestic sale. Anyone driving a car could be stopped at police roadblocks and asked to justify the reason for their journey; failure to provide a good answer could result in imprisonment or a hefty fine.

ADVICE FOR MOTORISTS

The government issued a broad range of advice about how to modify cars for blackout conditions. Stipulations given in 1940 included: use only one headlamp, fitted with a slit mask; reversing lights prohibited; white paint on the bumpers and running boards to increase visibility. A note on a poster also stated a precaution to prevent the car's possible use by an invading enemy: 'If the car is left outside, part of the mechanism must be removed, or a locking device applied, or the car must be in a locked garage or yard.'

Of course the alternative to car travel was rail, but here too there were limitations. The blackout applied to train carriages, with windows covered and light bulbs painted blue, and stations were completely blacked out, resulting in many people getting off at the wrong station. Train travel was restricted as the government had taken over the train companies, and most rail transport was dedicated to moving soldiers and war materials. The few public trains that ran became overcrowded, with passengers often having to stand for hours. For short journeys, therefore, it is little wonder that the horse and cart had something of a renaissance during the wartime years.

LEFT: It was not only road travel that was made more perilous by the blackout: seen here is the wreckage of a Scottish Express train that crashed into another train at Bletchley Station, Buckinghamshire, killing four people.

Smiling Through

Even in wartime, the British people still found time for fun. Music, cinema, dance and comedy became the pressure-release valves for an entire nation, even if some of the pastimes did not meet with official approval from the government or other moral censors.

Within the home, traditional games such as charades and bridge were now supplemented by the radio, with all but the poorest households owning a Bakelite wireless. The radio not only broadcast news but also immensely popular comedy shows. Most adored was *ITMA*, an abbreviation of 'It's that Man Again'. The man in question was Tommy Handley, and accompanied by a cast including actress Dorothy Summers he gave the British public a half-hour blast of odd-ball comedy every Thursday evening. Other comedy programmes included *Hi Gang* and *Happidrome*, but for those who wanted more intellectual entertainment there was always *The Brains Trust*, a programme in which an esteemed panel of academics debated a highbrow philosophical question.

Music, both live and over the airwaves, was also a big part of British life. On the radio, the BBC's *Music While You Work* show was broadcast every day at 10.30 a.m. and 3.00 p.m., often from public speaker systems in factories to break the tedium and drabness of the day. The songs of Vera Lynn both moved people to tears and made her a national heroine. Dance bands played to frequently huge crowds in halls around the country every Saturday night. The weekly dance could be a sparkling, vivacious affair, full of glamorous women and men in uniform, all swaying along to tunes

ABOVE: The members of radio show *ITMA* entertained millions of people every week with their off-beat comedy. Pictured (from left to right): Tony Francis, Derek Guyler, Molly Weir and Tommy Handley.

RIGHT: A dance given for British and US military personnel at Covent Garden Opera House in February 1944. Despite wartime austerity, the weekly dance could still be a time of fun, bright lights, warmth and good music.

THE FORCES' SWEETHEART

Vera Lynn was born in 1917 and began her singing career, aged only seven, in working men's clubs. Her talent was recognized well before the war, and she made radio recordings with popular big bands like the Joe Loss Orchestra. Yet during the war she was catapulted to stardom as a solo artist. Her songs, and her sincerity, struck a chord with the British public, and tunes such as 'We'll Meet Again', 'The White Cliffs of Dover' and 'Yours' virtually became national anthems. Known as 'the forces' sweetheart', Miss Lynn travelled the world to entertain troops with live concerts, enduring hardship and, at times, danger. Her shows in Burma in particular made British troops out there feel less forgotten. She continued to entertain after the war, and was awarded the OBE in 1969 and made a Dame of the British Empire in 1975.

ABOVE: George Formby was a popular entertainer and actor, known particularly for his risqué songs accompanied by the ukulele. Formby travelled to entertain troops in Europe and North Africa with ENSA (Entertainments National Service Association). After the war he was awarded an OBE for his services.

ABOVE: Vera Lynn became the voice of the wartime British generation. She ran a radio programme from 1940 entitled *Sincerely Yours*, in which she read out messages to and from British servicemen.

such as Glenn Miller's 'Moonlight Serenade' or Cole Porter's 'Don't Fence Me In'. For those less energetic, live classical concerts or piano recitals were often performed in local town or church halls.

Cinema provided another welcome diversion. The typical wartime cinema programme consisted of two films (a 'B' movie and the main feature) plus a newsreel and any government information film running at the time. The films ranged from stirring military dramas such as *In Which We Serve* (1942) through to popular Hollywood epics – *Gone With The Wind* (1939) was a particular favourite. Indeed, despite all the wartime restrictions, the British and American film industries ensured that there were plenty of new films to be seen, at least 500 between 1939 and 1945.

Dad's Army

On 14 May 1940 the government broadcast a radio message saying that it was forming a new volunteer, part-time military force for home defence known as the Local Defence Volunteers (LDV). It was open to all those too young or too old for regular military service (ages 17–65 were accepted), or who had been excluded from regular military service for other reasons, such as working in reserved occupations. The response was enormous. In only 24 hours, 250,000 men had volunteered, and more kept coming. By the end of May there were 750,000 members, and more than a million by the end of June. The LDV was renamed the Home Guard, and Britain had in place its very own volunteer army.

Popularly known as 'Dad's Army', the Home Guard at first inspired little confidence amongst onlookers. Initially most Home Guard units had no uniforms – just an armband to denote their service – and few firearms. The men were therefore encouraged to bring whatever weapons they could along to meetings, including personal hunting firearms, agricultural tools, various blades, lengths of pipe or broomsticks, or anything else from the cupboard that was potentially lethal. Training was also haphazard, typically delivered by volunteer commanders who had leadership experience from the First World War. Equipment and clothing did improve over time. Most men had basic army uniforms by the end of 1940, and US-supplied P14 and P17 rifles plus British Lee-Enfields were eventually issued.

Although the threat of invasion had subsided by mid 1941, the Home Guard was retained until December 1944. They were initially intended to act as a guerrilla force to fight an invading German army, but were put to good use in a variety of other roles – guard duty, manning roadblocks, helping with bomb disposal, assisting the emergency services. Some 140,000 Home Guard were also tasked with manning anti-aircraft batteries.

Their duties involved real danger – a total of 1,206 Home Guard soldiers were killed during the war, and 557 seriously wounded – and while history views them as rather eccentric, they rose to be a professional and essential part of Britain's defence infrastructure. Their contribution to Britain's defence was recognized by the monarchy, and on two occasions – 20 May 1941 and 20 May 1943 – the Home Guard was given the honour of mounting guard over Buckingham Palace. When they were finally disbanded,

BELOW: Improvisation was central to the Home Guard. This makeshift tank has been produced by attaching crude metal plates around a regular civilian car, and fitting a machine gun on the top.

LEFT: This soldier of the 25th Battalion, London Home Guard, has devised his own ingenious form of camouflage, using old strips of wallpaper. His firearm – a Thompson sub-machine gun – was a rarity amongst Home Guard forces, who more commonly held the Lee-Enfield rifle or civilian guns.

LEFT: Home Guard troops learn the principles of shooting at enemy aircraft, here simulated by a model gliding down wires. The Home Guard was not a substitute for the regular army, but it performed duties that relieved pressure on British Army forces.

on 3 December 1944, King George VI (Colonel-in-Chief of the Home Guard) stated that 'History will say that your share in the greatest of all our struggles for freedom was a vitally important one'.

It should be noted that the Home Guard were not the only volunteer military force in Britain. We have already seen various women's services, but another important formation was the Observer Corps. Again staffed by unpaid volunteers, the Observer Corps served to report on sightings or sound detections of German aircraft, particularly those that flew beneath British radar, or V1 flying bombs. Working from a total of 1,500 observation posts (by 1944) dotted around the country, the observers reported their sightings to control centres, which coordinated a fighter response. Like many Home Front duties the work could be dull but was vital, and was further evidence of the British people's commitment to protecting their nation and defeating Hitler.

RIGHT: The Air Transport Auxiliary (ATA) served to fly aircraft to bases around the UK, and its pilots not only included men who had been unable to join the regular RAF, but also women. Here a female officer (centre) walks away from her aircraft after a ferry flight.

Foreign Friends, Foreign Foes

Between 1940 and 1945, Britain effectively became a huge military base off the coast of mainland Europe, and by staying out of German hands made possible the Allied invasion of France in 1944. One side effect of this status, however, was that the island was to become home to the fighting men of many nations.

At first most of these new arrivals were combatants who had escaped from occupied Europe. They included nearly 140,000 French soldiers evacuated from Dunkirk, plus troops from Belgium, Czechoslovakia, the Netherlands, Norway, Poland and (later) Greece. The new arrivals gained the respect of their hosts – Czech and Polish fighter pilots, amongst others, fought and died in the RAF during the Battle of Britain – and many provided romantic diversions for British women. Sometimes the culture clash was all too painfully apparent – in one incident, a bailed-out Polish pilot, shot down fighting against an enemy air raid, was beaten to death by enraged Londoners who thought that he was German.

By far the biggest foreign influx into British shores was the Americans. The United States entered the war in December 1941, and from then until 1944 Britain became the major US base for prosecuting the war against Hitler in Europe. The US Eighth Air Force began deploying to Britain in 1942, bringing with it thousands of air crew and support personnel. This American influx intensified in the run-up to the D-Day landings in June 1944, for which vast numbers of US soldiers and sailors arrived in Britain for preparation and training. Some Americans were based in the UK for several years, and hence built up close ties with British civilians. Local feelings about them were mixed. Many women admired their good looks, charm, style (US uniforms were well-made, with a slender tailored fit), politeness – and affluence. The latter brought access to all the luxuries that Britain itself could not provide, including cosmetics, silk stockings and chocolate. Anglo-US romances blossomed in their thousands, contributing to a huge increase in divorces (25,000 in 1945) and a surge in illegitimate babies – it is likely that some 70,000 wartime babies were fathered by Americans. Most of these romances ended in eventual separation when the US soldiers were deployed, but thousands of women married and moved to the United States as 'GI brides' with their husbands following the war.

BELOW: Britain owes a debt of gratitude to the many displaced foreign fighter pilots who, flying aircraft such as the Supermarine Spitfire seen here, helped secure victory in the Battle of Britain. The pilot on the left is Polish fighter 'ace' Jan Zumbach.

LEFT: An African-American soldier dances with a woman from the WAAF. The US armed forces were still segregated at this time in history, and such sights could bring out racial tensions between black and white American soldiers.

For all of these reasons, Britain's menfolk were generally suspicious, or actively hostile, to the American forces. Unable to compete with their US counterparts in terms of appearance, glamorous aura and salaries – a British private earned just 14s (70p) a week, while a US equivalent earned £3 8s 9d (£3.44) – British soldiers feared that their wives or girlfriends would be drawn away by the visitors. The expression 'Over-sexed, over-paid and over here' summarized these concerns, but in balance the US troops were also capable of enormous generosity, organizing parties for children and bomb-hit communities. More importantly, they undeniably brought the means to win the war in the West.

ABOVE: Thousands of foreign prisoners of war were put to good work on Britain's fields. This group of POWs are assisting a British farmer and his son with haymaking.

POWS IN BRITAIN

Another foreign influx, as the war progressed, was huge numbers of German and Italian prisoners of war (POWs) – 400,000 Germans alone by the end of the war. Although they were initially kept separate from the population, their use as agricultural labourers brought steady integration. Prisoners were often taken out of their camps on social trips at the weekends, such as to see football matches or go to restaurants. Relationships, both friendly and romantic, were struck up between former enemies, the POWs often showing great kindness to local children, in part to control their own homesickness. Such was the fondness that many POWs felt for Britain that 26,000 of them became British citizens after the war.

Parliament and Royalty

In the British government, it was quickly realized that traditional party politics would not work in a conflict situation. What the country needed was unity, and that unity came in the form of one impressive leader – Prime Minister Winston Churchill.

At the beginning of the war, the incumbent Prime Minister, Neville Chamberlain, was head of the Conservative Party. Chamberlain's reputation had been damaged in his dealings with Hitler before September 1939, and Britain's poor performance fighting in Norway in 1940 led to a complete collapse in his authority. Both the opposition and many of his own supporters turned against him, and Winston Churchill took over on 10 May.

Churchill's leadership during the Second World War has become legendary. In charge of a coalition government (the 1940 general election was suspended), and with government given complete authority over the nation's activities, Churchill both inspired the people and made judicious strategic decisions. He was particularly renowned for his powers of oratory, which held up a nation demoralized by defeats and threatened by invasion. His presence was powerful, yet he could also be warm and funny, qualities that made him a supreme international statesman. Churchill committed the nation to resist the Nazis even when many wanted to capitulate or pursue appeasement, and for that reason the nation owes him a debt of gratitude.

ABOVE: On 30 September 1938, Prime Minister Neville Chamberlain returned from Munich, having agreed to allow the Germans to take over the Sudetenland portions of Czechoslovakia. He waved the agreement in the air, and famously declared that it represented 'peace for our time'.

RIGHT: A famous image of Prime Minister Neville Chamberlain preparing to announce the British declaration of war against Germany over the BBC airwaves, on 3 September 1939. Within nine months he would be replaced by Winston Churchill.

The other state authority was the Royal Family. By this point in history they were largely figureheads rather than leaders, but they had an important role in maintaining the morale of the nation. Many members of royalty and the nobility served in the armed forces; the young Princess Elizabeth even joined the ATS. Buckingham Palace was struck by bombs on several occasions and badly damaged, a situation that prompted Queen Elizabeth to say 'I'm so glad that we've been bombed. It makes me feel that I can look the East End in the face.' Royal visits to bomb-hit areas gave public morale a much-needed boost. Although both the Prime Minister and the Royal Family had moments when their popularity dipped, there was no denying that overall their presence helped shore up the nation's spirits.

CHURCHILL'S ORATORY

Churchill delivered dozens of inspiring speeches while in office. This is an extract from just one of them, delivered to the House of Commons on 18 June 1940, after France had fallen:

What General Weygand called the Battle of France is over. I expect that the Battle of Britain is about to begin. Upon this battle depends the survival of Christian civilization. Upon it depends our own British life, and the long continuity of our institutions and our Empire. The whole fury and might of the enemy must very soon be turned on us. Hitler knows that he will have to break us in this island or lose the war. If we can stand up to him, all Europe may be free and the life of the world may move forward into broad, sunlit uplands. But if we fail, then the whole world, including the United States, including all that we have known and cared for, will sink into the abyss of a new Dark Age made more sinister, and perhaps more protracted, by the lights of perverted science. Let us therefore brace ourselves to our duties, and so bear ourselves that, if the British Empire and its Commonwealth last for a thousand years, men will still say, 'This was their finest hour.'

ABOVE: King George VI and Queen Elizabeth inspect a cinema building in London wrecked by German bombing in 1940. The royal couple stayed in London throughout the Blitz.

BELOW: Prime Minister Winston Churchill addresses a large crowd shortly after the end of war in Europe in 1945. Churchill was an ideal war leader – resolute, intelligent, emotionally strong and able to handle criticism.

Victory

The war in Europe ended on 7 May 1945, with Germany's total and unconditional surrender. Japan also capitulated the following August. In Britain, the immediate reaction of many people was to throw some of the biggest parties the world had ever seen, with millions flooding onto the streets of villages, towns and cities in public displays of euphoria. For others, the surrenders brought sad reflections on those who were not alive to enjoy the day.

The end of the conflict did not alleviate austerity. Rationing continued in some form until the mid 1950s, with Britain exporting much of its produce in an attempt to pay for some of its enormous war debt. Socially, the biggest challenge was to find employment and purpose for four million soldiers as they were 'demobbed' (released from military service) and returned home. Wives and husbands, children and fathers had to readjust to each other after long periods of separation, often finding that their experiences had shaped them into very different people from those their families remembered. Divorces surged once again.

The war also reshaped Britain politically. In the 1945 general election Churchill's Conservatives were roundly defeated by Clement Attlee's Labour Party, which went on to create the National Health Service and the Welfare State. The Second World War, for many, showed Britain at its very best, a time in which everyone pulled together with resilience, humour and fortitude. The full picture, as we have seen, is slightly more complicated. Yet what is unquestionable is that the British people endured hardships present generations would find unimaginable, and did so with tenacity, courage and a largely unified spirit.

BELOW LEFT: A mass of joyful people crowd atop a van during the Victory in Europe (VE) celebrations. The end of the war brought celebrations, sadness for those not alive to enjoy them, and a new hope for the future.

BELOW RIGHT: Homecoming. Many soldiers returned from military service in 1945 to see children born while they were overseas. Here a British Army corporal holds his eight-month old daughter as he arrives back in England.